FUTURE PERFECT TENSE

An anthology of new writing

from

*Anglia Ruskin University's
Creative Writing MA*

First published in 2024 by
CAMBRIDGE WRITING CENTRE
Anglia Ruskin University
East Road
Cambridge
Cambridgeshire CB1 1PT

Typeset in Garamond and Raleway

Copyright of text and images remains with the authors.

All rights reserved.

No part of this book may be reproduced, stored in a retrieval system or transmitted in any form without the written permission of Sidekick Books.

Cover artwork by Lujain Al Thahabi
Typesetting by Jon Stone,
Jac Harmon and Emma Lister

ISBN: 978-1-909560-32-1

Contents

FOREWORD by Chris Beckett 7

LUJAIN AL THAHABI
   Hot Air Balloon 11

NICOLA COLLENETTE
   Fragile State 15

EMMA DU TOIT
   Footnote 25
   Divergent 26
   The Thing About Therapy 28

JAC HARMON
   Only the Dust 31

JEREMY HUBBARD
   Goodbye and Farewell 43
   The First Interview 50
   Need 54
   To Do Today: 55

EMMA LISTER
   Last Will & Testament 57

REBECCA OSTLER
- *Sting* *69*
- *for you* *73*
- *Summer* *74*

LISA SARGEANT
- *The Song of the Currawong* *77*

JOSHUA WOOD
- *Gold* *89*

Foreword

For some time now an annual pleasure of mine has been my guest lecture for ARU creative writing students, in which I try to persuade them of the many joys and benefits of writing within the conventions of science fiction. After I've said my piece, I set them the task of creating a setting for a science fiction story which would allow them to explore some theme, topic or idea which is meaningful to them. Given that it's only ever a minority of the group that has previously had any interest in this kind of fiction, I'm always impressed by the ideas that come up, ranging from bizarre to preposterous (both excellent qualities of course), to funny, to scarily plausible, to sorely tempting to pinch and use myself. (I do, of course, resist that temptation!)

So it's a pleasure but not a surprise to see the wide spread of different forms, subjects and styles of the present collection: poetry, travelogue, a last will and testament, microfiction (nanofiction, even?) ... and – yeeeessss! – several pieces of science fiction. These are gloomy times – a time when the hope that the world is heading towards something better can be very hard to sustain – and that's definitely reflected in the tone of most of these pieces, but even in dark places there's still room for playfulness and humour, and these are also very apparent here.

I'm guessing that, for some contributors, this will be the first time they've seen their own work in print. This is important moment for a writer. Writing is a strange ritual whereby we take things from inside ourselves, and shape them into something capable of a separate existence in the world outside. Seeing your own work in print can be a powerful confirmation that somehow you have achieved this apparently miraculous thing. I have been writing for many years, but I still sometimes open one of my books at random and ask myself 'Was this actually me? Did I really make this?' (I don't think it's egoism: it feels more like a kind of bewilderment!) I hope the writers represented here will look at their work in this collection and have that same experience – and I wish them many more such experiences in the years ahead.

— CHRIS BECKETT, May 2024

Lujain Al Thahabi

Lujain is a writer, one with ambitions to try and write as wide as the eye can see. She writes creative fiction inspired by cultures she'd like to know more about and dabbles in themes of nonconformity. Poetry has been an outlet for her thoughts for quite some time, as it allows her to challenge tradition and play with unexplored meanings. Her poem 'Hot Air Balloon' reflects on chasing yourself down as the future approaches, and how one deals with moving on from different versions of oneself.

Based in Cambridge, she aims to work on her short stories and poetry collection to bring colour to an otherwise mellow day.

Hot Air Balloon

A summer night
lasts longer than one would think,
as we run around in this sweltering heat,
patches of grass kissing our feet.

One by one
we tumble and fall and roll around,
like adults turned children or children turned adults,
sharing our 'what-ifs' and how far we'll float, how far we'll reach,
despite the snail's pace at which we move.

'Take your time!'
This gradually becomes a lie.
As these lush green fields web out,
and slow isn't fast enough,
we move,
and pitter, and patter, and wobble—

'I'll show you!'

As I leave you behind at dawn,
no desire to look back
at your young face, bruised heart and complaints,
your mean mouth that always knows what not to say.

At you,
the me I'm abandoning
for greater heights in this hot air balloon,
rising,
rising,

rising,
rising.

And depending on the weather,
perhaps even falling,
falling,
falling,
failing.

But that's for me to find out,
not you.
Because it's me,
not you,

in this hot air balloon.

Nicola Collenette

Ely-based Nic Collenette started writing about food, wine and travel as a journalist in Brighton. Since then, her escapades have included being the voice of Richard Branson, stomping grapes in the Douro and masquerading as a pub pundit on national radio. She completed her MA in Creative Writing in 2024.

Fragile State

'There's been one case of rabies in the village in the past ten years,' the leader of the trip reassured us at the first meeting. I'd seen the way feral dogs in India had reacted to me on previous visits. Hackles rising, teeth bared, rumbling growls. Pink tongues lolling out of the sides of foamy mouths. Rows of teats hanging low. Fearfully guarding their puppies from the approach of strangers. 'The dogs in the village tend to drive out those that aren't part of the pack,' the professor continued.

In that initial meeting on a winter's day in Cambridge, the eight staff and students from ARU, including me, had to confess what caused us the most anxiety about our forthcoming visit to a rural part of northern India. I had read previous participants' accounts and what resonated were the descriptions of creeping vampiric leeches. I'd come across those creatures, so lauded by the Victorians, while trekking in Sri Lanka. At first, I mistook them for harmless caterpillars, moving along at a brisk pace on the forest floor, their cartoonish, thin, inch-long black bodies folding in on themselves in a loop before stretching out again. When I pointed out their worm-like movements, my partner looked at me as if I was a fool, before haughtily correcting my woeful insect/invertebrate mix-up. He knew I feared those slimy bloodsuckers. Our Tamil guide had instructed us to cover our socks liberally with salt before heading out, to stop them inching up over our boots and legs. He pointed out that the leeches weren't going to spread any diseases and promised they were harmless enough. He took us to a waterfall deep in the rainforest where we swam in holy waters, and I managed to pinch one from in between my toes after it had sucked on my blood. I'd stayed calm enough, but the memory made me squirm.

This time, we would be setting off in the dry season so I believed the other member of staff coordinating the project when he told us that leeches shouldn't be so plentiful. I didn't mention my phobia of rats – the less talk about those disgusting vermin, the better.

It was to be my fifth trip to India. I'd applied to the scheme through work that New Year to escape the cold of the UK. The project, in conjunction with the Global Sustainability Institute at ARU, involved a homestay in a remote village in the sacred Hindu region of Uttarakhand. I knew that it would push me out of my comfort zone. My recent holiday to the south, taking in the modern tech hub of Bengaluru – the jungle at Nargarhole, the ancient cities of Mysuru and Madurai and the colonial town of Puducherry in Tamil Nadu – had been relatively relaxed. My sense of taste had emerged again after a first bout of coronavirus and I'd made the most of the fluffy array of oil-smothered breads, toothachingly sweet pak – similar to fudge but perhaps made with even more sugar – and sumptuous vegetarian thalis served on bright green banana leaves instead of a plate.

In contrast, this next venture to the north promised to be exhausting. I'd seen the photos of drained-looking students – heads in hands and sitting on the side of a dusty road after a couple of weeks of hard graft, lingering jet lag and long days. We would teach English in the village school and provide first aid advice for residents in neighbouring villages. The university group was a mix of ages and backgrounds – some medical students, others in construction management. My research had uncovered that Uttarakhand means 'northern land' in Sanskrit and has long been associated with myth and mountains. It is split into two districts: Garhwal and Kumaon.

The western region of Garhwal, where we were staying in Sainji village – famous for its corn growing – is the burly half of the state, due to its 'masculine' terrain. The character of the landscape is defined by four rivers flowing from Himalayan glaciers, carving the terrain into a tight-knuckled network of ridges and canyons.

We were picked up by local Garhwali taxi drivers at Indira Gandhi International Airport, rather than Delhi taxis unused to the treacherous roads, and I was glad I'd had the foresight to pack copious supplies of travel pills. As soon as the crags of the Himalayas were in sight, the road snaking through the mountains became nerve-wracking and stomach-churning, despite my medication.

After seven hours' driving (covering around 300 kilometres), we reached the hill station town of Mussoorie, where a landslide half an hour earlier had left traffic at a standstill. One parked car had been crushed under fist-sized rocks packed in like in a dry-stone wall and two others were teetering precariously on the edge of the road above us. I'd read that monsoon-season landslides could block roads, but now unseasonable heavy rainfall had dissolved the sides of the mountain into tumbling rubble.

We drove past JCBs digging out cars from potholed roads torn up by the storm. I imagined we might be driving through the aftermath of a warzone. It was frightening to witness the ecological fragility of the Himalayas so dramatically. The professor explained that a lot of the landslides were down to deforestation. She said that the structure of the geology of the young mountains could be likened to ripples in a carpet. This part of the Himalayas in Mussoorie was the first of five more huge ravines that had been slammed into place when the India landmass first moved from the South Pole and crashed into Asia. That mountain-range concertina was the first zigzag, after which the crags were pushed up higher and higher. Small hamlets clung on to the rockface – all precariously built in earthquake-prone zones. Everest was the highest ripple in neighbouring Nepal – around 1,000 km to the east, as the crow flies.

I learnt that a terrible crash on the Mussoorie road two years earlier had resulted in a woman being thrown from her seat 100 metres down a ravine. Incredibly she had survived and only had a broken leg. She had lain there overnight and the next day she and her husband, who was still in the overturned car, were found by a villager who heard their cries. The driver had some crushed vertebrae but both were still alive after he took a corner too fast. Now a flimsy-looking metal barrier marked the spot.

We drove on in the taxi past an enormous waterfall at Kempty, the stream far heavier than usual due to the deluges over the last couple of days. Everyone carried on as normal, dressing up in gaudy Rajasthani-style clothes for the tourists, who stood in front of static photos of the waterfalls to create perfect pictures and memories. My friend remarked that these were for the husbands to point at in the future when their wives said they never went anywhere. We pushed on over potholed roads for another 15 kilometres until we finally reached the corn village. It was a little underwhelming at first after more than 24 hours of travelling. We were dropped off at a dark, open-walled structure with a lone scruffy puppy to welcome us as we unfolded ourselves from the cab.

It felt like a multi-storey car park, with a concreted floor and all the fustiness of a dank corridor. My spirits lifted as the sun came out from behind the clouds and we made our way through the village square, which was decorated with golden cobs of corn, past traditional houses daubed with red hearts against a rich blue paint. I breathed in the clear air, smelling ozone and hearing the *kri-kri* call of parakeets flying low overhead. No honking horns here. A lemon tree was in bloom and its scent drifted along the trickling channel of water used to irrigate the fields of wheat, the waterway made from ancient-looking stone and slippery underfoot.

Four of us shared a low-ceilinged village home, made from deodar wood – Himalayan cedar – with small doors believed to keep evil away. The spiders were the biggest challenge – huge black beasts jumping out of their lairs and making us all jump in tandem. These spiders were poisonous; last year a staff member was rushed to hospital for antivenom medication after a nasty reaction to a bite on the back of his neck.

Fortunately, this year no one was attacked. Our room had two single beds in it and a day-bed next to the cupboards from which the spiders crept every evening and to which they returned by morning. I didn't dare look inside.

It was colder than expected in the hills. Dark rolling clouds and the unusual rainfall cooled off the heat of the sun. A rainbow greeted us on the first afternoon, high over the chiselled mountains surrounding the village, the sharp smell of pine drifting after the rain. From the roof of the homestay, I saw steep terraced fields, the lush green crops reminding me of Bali. There were no rice paddies: land was for growing corn and wheat.

Further down into the valley lay abandoned villages. A 1,000-metre trek down to the river Aglar, home to a boisterous annual fish festival, revealed empty houses given up for an easier life away from the hardships of farming. Enormous new hydro dams in the area had caused more ecological harm to the fragile peaks amid ribbons of land-clearing, but had brought electricity to the people in the neighbouring city of Dehradun, and as far as Delhi.

We organised a nature walk with the village schoolchildren so that we could get an opportunity to learn from them, while they practised their English speaking and listening. We walked together past huge sheets laid out on dusty floors, on top of which fresh turmeric dried out. The familiar earthy smell complemented the sweet, spicy chai gifted to us by older sisters and graduates of Sainji's school. The children were excited and rowdy away from their desks, proud to show off their knowledge of the different plants growing wild along the road. They were aghast when told the price of curry leaves in the UK and insisted we take armfuls home with us. I enquired about snakes and the students confirmed that they were common. A chatty ten-year-old girl with pale blue eyes told me with relish about how she killed venomous kraits by whacking them on the head. We walked past the original water source for the village – still the preferred drinking spot of some elders who didn't trust the water that came out of the tap.

The children pointed at short wooden stakes wrapped in red or white string. I went to take a video of the picturesque scene after I noticed a black-and-white forktail bird, but the students looked anxious and told me not to – they didn't want me to have any record on my phone of the wooden stakes protecting them against the evil eye. They pushed forward a fellow student who had a solid black circle next to her eyebrow – I'd noticed these before and wrongly thought they were birthmarks. It was drawn on by her family to ward off evil spirits. The thin pieces of string wrapped around the wood were believed to rid the villagers of hexes put on them by other people. If they were undone – or even acknowledged in a recording – bad luck would come.

On our return to school, we came across a bamboo house standing empty, built by the government without consultation, for use as a guesthouse, with breathtaking views across the valley, purple peaks stretching far into the distance. The villagers saw it as a dangerous presence full of ghosts: no one claimed it and it belonged to nobody.

We met with two older women later that night who told us of the benefits of change in the village. They remembered when there was no electricity and reflected that life was easier for them now. Two of the girls from the university were fluent in Hindi and translated for us, as the women spoke no English. One talked of getting married at age eleven and having her first child when she was fifteen. She had gone on to have a further two sons and four daughters, but the eldest one had since died of tuberculosis.

They told us about another friend of theirs, who was eight when she got married to an eleven-year-old boy. She was widowed at 21. They said that they'd never been to school and didn't know how old they were. The women still cut grass for oxen by hand and grew peas, corn and wheat every season, despite being bent over double, hands crippled by arthritis. My friend told me about her grandfather, who knew the rough year and month of his birth. She explained that his records were destroyed after Partition, so each sibling in his family had an official birthdate of 1900, rather than 1936 in his case.

We heard from the women about polygamy in the village, now illegal. They saw it as a practical way for women to be protected in case of death. Once married, there would be Big Papa, usually the eldest son. His brothers would be called Middle Papa and Little Papa depending on their age. One wife married all the brothers, and they lived together in one of the lone traditional houses we had seen dotted through the village, an upper floor serving as the communal living area, with grain stored below. Another wife might be brought in for additional help, or if there hadn't been any children produced. The old women told us about a man they knew who took seven wives and received a dowry each time, but none of his brides ever fell pregnant. They laughed that he grew rich from his barren wives, even though it was he who clearly couldn't have children.

We found out that one of the old women sharing her experiences with us was related to the eighteen-year-old woman providing us with delicious dhal, rice and vegetable curries each day. We asked about the ages of her relatives and discovered that the woman we'd been talking to was in her mid-fifties. With her toothless mouth, she appeared thirty years older.

A weekend trip to the holy city of Rishikesh had been organised in favour of an overnight trek to the peak of Nag Tibba to witness the sunrise. This decision was made after we learned the wild camping trip involved a nine-hour car journey, temperatures of -6°C and heavy snowfall. We headed to Rajbagh village in the middle of Rajaji National Park instead, a four-hour drive from Sainji. We taught the schoolchildren and their parents how to treat burns, help people who were choking and stem blood flow from cuts using a scarf and a stick for a tourniquet.

There was no electricity in the village and the women told us they followed their cows to get back home and lit fires to ward off jackals and leopards. Later, back in Rishikesh, we attended Aarti as dusk fell. The picturesque city was much-loved by the Beatles and was now a huge yoga hub. I learnt that Ganga Aarti was perhaps the most important event related to the holy river and involved the chanting of hymns, accompanied by fire, flowers and swathes of worshippers. The sound of mantras was haunting and hypnotic, accompanied by the musky smell of incense and drums and bells played by monks in saffron robes.

I woke early back in Sainji, with jet lag and my sleep affected by the midnight visitations of a rat in the homestay. The fact that I'd managed to fall asleep again after seeing that vermin (one of my worst nightmares) was proof that I was toughening up. The earlier-than-usual start was rewarded by the oscillating call of an Indian roller bird, growing higher and higher in pitch with each cry. Its large wings flashed a beautiful iridescent blue against the dawn.

There was a moan that sounded like someone in pain. An old woman sat outside the homestay, bent double, crying and rocking, surrounded by other villagers looking on. I guessed that she was mourning and found out later there had been an unexpected death in the family. That week another villager had also passed away 'from old age'. We had been alerted to two additional medical emergencies in the village, which my paramedic friend had been asked to deal with. The families were unwilling to go to the hospital, partly due to the fact it took at least an hour by car – something they had no access to – and partly due to cost. One was a middle-aged man suffering from a botched operation at a government hospital that had led to sepsis and the other a similarly-aged man with a suspected aneurysm, who'd been unable to get checked as he had no one to look after his goats.

My fellow student felt helpless, with only a rudimentary first-aid kit available, and advised them to get to the closest private hospital, but her instruction at first went unheeded. A few days later we learnt that family rifts had been healed, thanks to her professional opinion, and both men were taken to hospital by relatives who owned cars. They were now on the mend back at their homes.

On my return to the UK, a friend asked me about the impact of our work in the village. I thought about small changes like these that we'd achieved, together with raising money for a retaining wall to protect the school from the inevitable monsoon landslides resulting from climate change. I reflected on the deep sense of satisfaction the group felt from our shared and learned experiences. Our trip to

India will stay with me as profoundly rewarding and a privilege – an opportunity I hope to repeat in the future.

Emma Du Toit

Emma has been writing poetry for the last 30 years. She has a cat, a chronic vitamin D deficiency and the usual number of insecurities for a 21st century woman waist-deep in perimenopause. Conversation starters she would rather avoid include: *Where are you from? Why are you late?* and *Tell me about the novel you're writing.*

Belonging, identity and fitting in are themes that recur within her work as she explores relationships between people, places and moments in time. Drawing on her own experiences, the poems included here examine the process of starting to belong following decades of having to fit in, connecting with your core self and discovering who you really are.

Footnote

Ways of looking at a fire: hold a clear prism in slippery fingers, one eye closed, one an emerald hidden in the rushes. Snuggle your breath into the branches of your lungs

Fold crepe sentences into backstories that ignite, sending embers spinning into eras as your voice becomes a generation of sound. Hushes, soothes, frays at the edges until your anecdotes hang like smoke in summer air

Divergent

In 1985 I borrowed *The Aristocats* on VHS so many times that the rental shop gave me the tape
The sticker on the front bore faded orange smudges where the letters had been worn away

I swam often through juddering pinks and purples into the streets of Paris
Muscle memory mouthing

    — *Poor Madame will be so worried.*

I became a sleeping kitten wriggled into pyjamas at the airport gate
Questing for home – snuggled in the back of a car – counting streetlights and the tops of trees…

    — *What's gonna happen to us, mama?*

We carried plastic bags of books between schools
Curated sepia photographs in albums
Moments that could have been dreams
Fleeting lives lived in rapid succession
Remember that dress?
Who's that girl?
This must have been the year we left…

I rode the waves, washing up on a new shore amongst flotsam, jetsam, salty rubble
Hopped through traffic to the next island
Left imprints of myself in so many lives and places

Racks of personalities on broken hangers
Itchy at the seams

I am looking forward
Moving on
Diverging

The Thing About Therapy

Don't laugh. My therapist was adamant about that. No one finds this funny. Except you. You're using humour and it's distracting.

It was the 11th session of 12 and I felt like Lina deserved a breakthrough. She was neither triumphant nor amused. I felt detached from my own body.

I'd walked around with barbed wire in my stomach, muscles aching with the effort of clenching myself into the shape of an acceptable human. Then suddenly I dropped it all. It's a cliché to say I flatlined but that's how I felt. I was down on one level; just a cool surface to lay my cheek against.

Sure, you can work through things, change your perspective on events, but ultimately the facts remain. Shame is like that dye they use in security vans and bank vaults. Even if you look clean on the outside, in the right light your crime will be revealed.

What's important in the world of therapy is to look cured. Then they'll leave you alone. Say the right things. Don't act mad. Don't share too much of your crazy. Let it seep gently into the chair cushion but try not to leave a wet patch.

Jac Harmon

Jac describes herself as a discovery writer who mostly writes historical-paranormal fiction, but isn't scared to try any genre or style. She lives in a world of her own near Cambridge with her husband and son, in a house haunted by the ghosts of her four cats: Muffin, Cookie, Willow and Steve.

Only the Dust

> *Even snow*
> *knows it's unclean. Each flake makes its own geometry*
> *around dust, where everything begins.*
>
> from Traci Brimhall: 'Dear Eros'.

Out here there is only the dust.

Don't rush, she says, take your time. Take a long, slow, breath. You are standing at the peak of a mountain beneath a blue sky. The air is clean and fresh. You feel exhilarated.

I hear this via my helmet's hearing loop. I would rather listen to music, something harsh, but Dr Walker's calm, unhurried tones are part of my training schedule. I follow her instructions as I walk, unsure of the efficacy of such exercises. Having never experienced mountain peaks, blue skies or clean, fresh air, they feel pointless. Here, the air is full of microscopic particles. Nasty things Dr. Walker would not want invading her lungs. From the safety of her sterile lab, she can afford to sound calm.

  Hard to believe there was a time before all this. When environmental terrorists were climate activists and dictatorships were democracies, and total control was climate control. Before money quashed protest and the planet's death knell rang out: the dull clang of a million empty promises. This is history and I do not think about it. I suspect Dr. Walker does not either, cocooned as she is by her privilege.

It is difficult to know where to direct my anger. At the World Science Corporation, under whose auspices I was originally employed? At Planetary Resources? Who, after five months of diligence, inform me the Transatlantic Dustbowl is beyond redemption and no action will be taken to improve air quality. Rage tests every ounce of my self-control as any complaint would risk my career progression; even my life. I can only monitor this dead zone, and feed back information to the descendants of those who perpetrated the catastrophe, safe within their insulated northern cities.

I shut Dr Walker down. I'm in no mood for training modules. Besides, what is fresh air? To keep myself from screaming I think of something else. I think of before. Tigi. Slouching in his chair with his feet on the desk. Eating real food you needed to chew. I remember how, when we worked together, I would tell him the stuff they churned out in the backstreets would probably kill him. I remember how he never listened. Thinking of Tigi raises my spirits, briefly.

A bleep in my ear warns me my time outside is over. It is a relief. I have had my fill of the never-ending dust range – all that is left of the Atlantic Ocean. Rather my grim glass-and-metal bunk room than the silicon eddies that sweep across this long-dead, once-sub-marine world.

I walk, head down. My boots make long, red scuffs in the desiccated surface. I feel the mounting tension of a storm in my shoulders. A glance reveals a leaden darkness gathering on the horizon. Forks of lightning joining land and sky, of a density and magnitude unusual enough to call in. I tighten my hood and switch channels on my hearing loop just as a marauding gust punches me in the back and knocks me off balance.

I stagger, saying, 'Lola to Comms.'

There is a long, low crackle, then: 'Comms to Lola. Where are you?' It is Kristoff.

'South West of Monitor 15.'

We both forget protocol, our voices strained.

'Reporting storm type 40 rising.'

'No shit.'

There is another long, low crackle. My buds die.

'Kristoff?'

I learned to deal with emptiness long before I was deposited at this arse end of nowhere, but I need the sound of his voice.

'Lo? Can you …' Static screeches deafen me.

'Kris — '

His name gets trapped in my mouth as the storm lifts me from my feet.

I switch to survival mode: curl into a ball, drop to the ground, and when the wind draws its next breath I flatten myself. I must not panic. I stay low expecting a blast of hot, granular dust, but instead I am blanketed with cold and my limbs ache.

'Lo?' My headset crackles as radio contact resumes, and the shock initiates movement. I begin to crawl. Whatever covers the ground is difficult to traverse and the temperature is dropping. My brain struggles to comprehend my situation even as my body moves automatically. *Frozen water*, it says. *Snow*. But there is no water here, and has not been for half a millennium. I lift a hand and stare at it. Stare ahead of me into a white wind. I begin to laugh.

#

Kristoff is waiting when I come out of decontamination. I have peeled off three layers of clothing, including a thick-wadded outer layer. It hangs in the ante-chamber like a flayed skin.

'Are you ok?'

I nod and look back again. 'It's cold outside,' I say, but he is already walking away toward the main control room. Halfway there, I stop and stare at the docking stations.

'Where are the shuttles?'

He is two steps ahead of me.

'Gone. The station's been abandoned.'

The shock is physical. It sucks the air from my lungs. Kristoff comes back and takes my arm. It's the first time he has ever touched me. It feels wrong.

'All three of them?'

'Fear ran through the crew like lightning when we lost contact with the World Science Corporation .'

'Even Dr. Horner? He was our chief. He should have stayed.'

'He took the first shuttle.'

There had been twenty of us. Scientists and support staff. Kristoff sits me in a chair in front of a dead terminal and stands behind me.

'I am glad you made it back.'

His face, reflected in the screen, says otherwise.

#

Later, when I am alone, I stand on the observation deck and press my cheek against the huge window, feeling the freeze. Outside, everything is white and newly contoured. I shiver, scared by the changes in both the environment and Kristoff. He has been secretly moving about the building when he thinks I am asleep, leaving me alone for long periods, then exploding into the silence.

A door slams and I tear my cheek from the glass, leaving behind fragments of skin.

Spinning around, my heart thundering, I see Kristoff running toward me. He is grinning like a loon and I swear at him. He skids to a stop.

'What?'

'You almost gave me a heart attack.'

'Sorry.'

'Where have you been?'

He begins to speak at top speed. A stream of space-boy jargon. I wave my hands, but there is no stopping him.

'What do you think?' he asks. 'Should we go below?'

I am wary, but agree, and follow him through a series of now-unsealed doors to a lift where he flashes a security card – I do not ask whose – and we descend to Lower Level 6.

When the doors open we step out into a maze of grey corridors and walk until I am disorientated. He stops and says, 'World Science Corporation: Information Vault 104. Weather reports for this sector for the last 500 years.'

He punches in a code and the door slides open. Old technology, preceding both fingerprint and iris recognition.

'You know the security codes?'

'I overrode them.' He grins. 'I had to do something while you were out monitoring. No one else spoke to me, and you only now and then.'

Is he trying to make me into a monster? And why now? My suspicions grow.

'Welcome to Dr Horner's lair.'

I step inside, into the dim glow of orange low-emission lighting. Time shifts. There are banks of metal filing cabinets and a central table covered with files – all dust-free, indicating Horner has been at work on these. I am captivated, but glad when we take armfuls of them and return to the observation deck. It will be far easier to work in the light filtering in through the great windows than under these faint bulbs.

#

We read. For hours. For days. Kristoff continues to make his night-time forays. During one of these I find a file hidden beneath his blankets. The more I read, the sicker I feel. I am not safe. Kristoff is not an ally.

I study charts, temperature readings, projections. Horner knows about the changes and has been planning all this since he first arrived. And then, when I am about to slip the file away, I discover the money. The names of those involved. And there is Dr Walker. Even she will live in this new, clean place. I feel sick. It has to stop. If there is hope for the future on this fucking planet, it is going to be hope for all. I will make sure of it.

I return the file, heart pounding, body shaking. On quiet feet I follow the auto-lights through Corridor Seven. Planetary Resources creaks around me, familiar noises, now joined by the groans of the ice moving. I know Kristoff often slips off to Meds V: Minor Injuries. A soft stream of light issues from the open door to illuminate the corridor, and a tapping sound tells me he is using a terminal. The bastard is communicating with the outside world.

#

I wake early to the sound of the Earth groaning and throw off my blankets, rushing to join Kristoff at the window. The white has divided itself to reveal a slash of blue, so bright I shade my eyes.

The colour is so astounding my emotions are uncontrollable. I stare until my eyes ache and tears flood my cheeks. I am, it appears, overcome.

Another groan, and this time the building moves – a sideways lurch that throws me against a desk. Kristoff has disappeared. Did he go below? When I reach the lift I lie on the floor and listen. I hear the building still shifting, trying to settle, and I feel the suck of sleep, but there are new voices. I wonder if I am hallucinating? I am not.

'How much longer?' Kristoff's voice.

'A day, maybe two.' Dr. Horner.

My breath catches.

Then a third voice I do not recognise. 'What about her?'

'Leave her to me.' Kristoff again.

My heart jumps like a jackhammer in my chest and I back away down the corridor until the voices are swallowed by the distance.

Everything is in its place when he returns, and I feign relief. A small movement in the ice, the glacier, he tells me. And then …

'Look, Lola, I found books.'

He drops his offering on a desk and I hide my face in the pages of a volume of eighteenth-century geological practices.

A few minutes pass.

'I was considering,' I say, turning to the window, 'taking a trip outside to test the air quality.'

He thinks this is a good idea. Treats everything as normal.

#

I am prepared for change, but not such radical change. I take every reading twice, wait thirty minutes, then take a third. The air is not only breathable but shows a level of purity I have never seen. Beneath my feet, the substance I now know to be snow glitters in the light from the sky rift. After checking my oxygen tank I leave my equipment in the airlock and set out for the bluff, eager to see the dust bowl under this great white shroud.

The contours of the landscape are unrecognisable. Great white waves have frozen in place but I am guided by the bluff itself: a navigational needle pointing due north. Climbing the hills is difficult in my suit and I stand atop the first mound to catch my breath and look down into the bowl, where my eye catches a flash of red. Sliding down to it, I brush away the crystalline top layer, and …

A scream escapes my throat, fogging my mask, and I scramble backward, upward, only to slide back down again. A face I recognise stares back at me. It is Bartlemy! I brush at the snow. Frantic. They are all there – every person Kristoff said had fled. I do not want to look at them. I do not want them to look at me.

When I return, Kristoff is off roaming the lower levels, so I check the terminal in Meds V. A couple of taps reveals Kristoff's part in Horner's plan for a rich person's paradise. Project Phoenix, the flower-covered sales brochure announces, will be created in a new temperate zone as the Earth tilts and assumes new weather patterns. I send everything to the Pan-World Environmentalists. It is imperative I do this before matters escalate. Before something happens to me.

In the meantime, and because it will arouse no suspicion, I continue to watch the widening blue sky and experience a deeper connection to the old Earth. Not in a clinical manner, but in a visceral way. Having found boxes of stationery (pencils, paper, erasers) I turn full analogue and write of clear air and clean water, using words of regeneration and a better future. When Kristoff returns, he is uninterested, and I begin to feel a disaster evolving into an opportunity.

#

It is my turn to play saboteur. Sixteen people lie dead beneath the ice and I will avenge them. Kristoff believes I know nothing, and I continue to play along. As he sleeps I monitor his messages. Horner and Rees, the First Engineer, (who I now know is the third voice I heard), are leaving on the only functioning shuttle tomorrow to collect their fellow conspirators from one of the bubble cities on the Siberian tundra. Using the terminal in Meds V I have contacted the Pan-World Environmentalists and they will wait beyond the bluff to destroy the shuttle. Kristoff, they will leave to me. I have assured them I am capable. My stomach roils when I think of what I must do but I only have to close my eyes and see those faces under the ice to know I am capable.

The traitor sleeps deeply. I find it insulting he is not more cautious, that he thinks so little of me, but it is to my advantage. I receive my final communication from the Pan-World Environmentalists and erase all contact. Now my own plan is in place I feel strange flickers of excitement. One day this place will be a new settlement, with people, plants and animals, where all might come to live. All I need do is kill a man.

I tell Kristoff about my findings, say the air quality is such that we can go outside without suits. He agrees at once and I wonder when he will reveal himself.

'Shall we walk up to the Dust Bowl?' he asks.

'Why not?'

We trudge through a fresh layer of snow. My footprints from the previous day have been filled so my discovery will remain a secret. Nevertheless, I take a different path – one which leads to a weather station equidistant from the PR building and the first of what were once underwater ranges. My teeth chatter as I attempt to second-guess what he means to do. At the top of a ridge we stop. He is gasping. Less fit than I. White peaks stretch before us, glittering in the new light that pours from the sky. If he is going to kill me, I think, it will be here. But he stands and stares, gets his breath back, and marvels at the sight. Then, with a look at his timepiece, he suggests we start back.

We are outside the airlock when he says, 'I'm sorry, Lola.'

My heart skips. This is it, but when I look he holds no weapon.

'I'm going to have to lock you out here.'

'Don't be an idiot, Kristoff. I'll freeze.'

He steps between me and the door. He has the advantage of size.

'That's the idea, Lola. I don't want to do it, but …'

He shrugs, and like an idiot, spreads his empty hands. I am on him. Whipping the geologist's pick from beneath my jacket, I bring it down on his left clavicle. There's a crunch of bone and he screams, collapsing to his knees.

'What the fuck!' He tries to rise, but my next swing takes him in the temple and there is no more talk. Easy, in the end, when it is you or them. I hit him again, but he has already stopped twitching.

Time passes. I have no idea how much, but the cold is creeping up through the soles of my feet, cramping my calves. From over my shoulder comes a roar. I turn to see a craft rise from a far-away repair facility: Horner and Rees setting off only to come face to face with a Pan-World cruiser. There is a flash and as the light fades, I watch the shuttle skitter across the ice, a plume of smoke rising into the sky behind it. Sparks explode where it skates across unblemished snow leaving a double sweep of curving tracks. When it reaches the bluff its nose dips and its tail rises. There is a brief pause before it drops from view and a thunderous explosion makes me stagger. The whole sky lights up and hot smoke encloses me. Wearing an oxygen mask again, I stand unmoving until the air clears and silence returns.

It is over. I drop the pick. Kristoff's blood has sketched scarlet roses in the snow in a place where one day real roses will bloom.

Jeremy Hubbard

Jeremy wrote his first short story at age nine, and has been a keen scribbler, on and off, ever since. He writes novels, novellas, short stories, poems and songs. He has had five short stories and several poems published to date, and is working on a novel series and a short story collection.

Jeremy has co-authored an alternative history novel, *The Hammer & The Anvil* (published by Arima Press) and originated, written and designed a mixed-media artwork in book form, *Towards an Understanding of Gravity* (published by WriteDesign).

Jeremy is neurodivergent and mostly straight. He lives in Cambridge with his wife and their dog and three cats. He has one daughter and two step-sons, now living in Halesworth, Amersham and Richmond.

Goodbye and Farewell

'Hello? Yes, hello? Hell–'
'Thank you for your enquiry. Your call is important to us. Please hold the line while we try to connect you.'
'Hello. Yes. My name is Mrs M. Smythe. Maude Sm–'
'An operator is not available at present. Please listen carefully to the options listed, then select the service you require using your keypad.'
'I don't have a keypad. This–'
'To book a local journey, press 1.'
'–is a telephone, not one of those lap computers.'
'To book a longer-distance journey, press 2.'
'I don't know what to do.'
'To cancel a local journey, press 3.'
'Do you mean for me to dial these numbers–'
'To cancel a longer-distance journey, press 4.'
'–on the front of my telephone?'
'If you would like to provide feedback on this or any other service we offer, please press 9. Your opinion matters to us.'
'Well, that's nice to know. At least there's that.'

Maude peers down at the beige carcass of her landline telephone; it squats like a toad on the curved shelf beneath the mirror in the hall. As she deliberates over the outsized numbers on the extra-large buttons designed for the visually impaired, she keeps the receiver pressed firmly to her ear.

'We are sorry. We were not able to register your response. Please try again. Please select the service you require, using your keypad.'
'But I don't know how.'
'To book a local journey, press 1.'
'Oh, for pity's sake!'
'To book a longer-distance journey, press 2.'

'Surely if I dial a number–'

'To cancel a local journey, press 3.'

'–it'll think I want to make another c–'

'To cancel a longer-distance journey, press 4.'

'–call and it'll cut me off?'

'If you would like to provide feedback on this or any other service we offer, please press 9. Your opinion matters to us.'

'Well, yes. I rather think I do.'

Leaning on the shelf, she huffs, sighs, shuffles her feet.

'We are sorry. We were not able to register your response. If you are unsure which service you require, press zero, then hold the line while we try to connect you to an operator, who will be happy to assist you. Your call will be placed in a queue.'

'Right, that's it: I'm dialling oh.'

Maude pokes her crooked forefinger down firmly onto the 'phone's big zero button. She hears a loud beep, followed by a soft purr, then:

'Your call is in a queue. Please hold the line while we try to connect you.'

'Oh, it seems to have worked. Bill would have been most impressed,' Maude addresses her reflection in the curlicue-framed mirror. She smiles nervously – unsure if the blotches are behind the glass or in front of it – and listens to a tinny rendition of Vivaldi's 'Winter'.

'Oh, that's nice,' she says. 'One of my favourites. Bill used to love *The Four Seasons*. How did you know?'

After a few bars, the music is interrupted by a beep.

'Your call is <second> in the queue. Please continue to hold, your call is important to us. Have you considered booking your ride online? You will find it quicker and easier.

To book your ride on-line, go to double-u, double-u, double-u dot, book my ride dot com, click on the journey-type you want, select date and time from the menus provided, input your full name, address and contact number, and input the location you want to travel to.'

'Input? No, that's okay, thank you. I don't do things online. I'll just carry on ... holding.'

'Alternatively, you can download our booking app onto your mobile device. It is free of charge and very easy to use.'

'No, thank you. I don't have a mobile device, whatever that might be.'

'Just scan the QR code from our website.'

'I don't know what one of those is, either. I don't do computers and web things. I am only partially sighted, you know, and it's getting worse. I can't see well enough to–'

Another beep, then:

'Your call is <first> in the queue. Please continue to hold, your call is important to us.'

'Yes, I rather suppose it is. Please would you play the music again?'

She greets the resumption of canned Vivaldi with a relieved smile. After a few more bars, it's cut off again, replaced by a cacophony of clanking and rattling.

'Hello. Yes, hello. Is anyone there, please? Hell–'

'Ah, yes, hello, er, Madam. I hope you're having a good day.'

'Well, no, not really. I–'

'Oh, dear, I am sorry to hear that. How can I help you? I assume you'd like to book a ride in one of our cars?'

'Yes, please. And I'm afraid it's rather urgent, now. You see–'

'Local?'

'Yes, to the hospital. You see, someone I know – very well, I like to think – she is going to–'

'Okay. Your address?'

'Oh, yes. It is eighteen – that is: one eight, not eight oh – so it's 18, Gardenia Row, off Coleman's Drive, West Dodsbury. And that's NR–'

'Yep. I've got you. Drove past there myself, recently.'

'Oh, jolly good. Now, can I make that a return, please?'

'No, sorry, Madam. We only do one-way tickets. You can call us again in the event that you need another ride.'

'Really? Goodness me. Well, I–'

'Name, please?'

'What – *mine?*'

'Yes – yours, please.'

'I already told you, at the beginning of this call.'

'No, Madam, you didn't.'

'I can assure you I did.'

'Honestly, I can assure you you didn't ... really.'

'But I did. I did. I–'

'Okay. Let's just say I forgot, then. Sorry for that; please tell me again.'

'Hhmph. Well, alright. It's Mrs Maude Smythe – with a Y.'

'Right. Time and date?'

'Today. Now. As soon as you can, please. I don't think there's much time left; they said things were likely drawing to a close, and it's important I can–'

'Right you are, Maude. Don't worry, I reckon I can get a car to you in about ten minutes, assuming you'd be happy with our standard vehicle and service.'

'I think so. What else could it be?'

'A limo.'

'A what?'

'A limousine. Posher, longer. Splash of luxury, polished leather, satin padding, varnished rosewood etc. Naturally, they cost more, and I couldn't get one to you for at least half an hour or so ...'

'Oh. No, dear, I don't think I could afford one of those, thank you. And anyway, an ordinary car will do just fine for little old me, as long as it gets here soon.'

'Right you are. You can pay for it by credit card or debit card now, or with cash at the end of your journey.'

'Cash, thank you. Oh, and–'

'You know, it would have been a lot easier, for both of us if you had booked your ride online. You can even pay for it online.'

'Well, as I already told you, I don't do computers, or internet, or mobile things, partly because I simply cannot see well enough.'

'No, Madam, you d– mmm, okay. I understand.'

'This has been fine for me, anyway, talking to you like this.'

'Lucky you timed it when you did, then – next week, we're going all automated. If it'd been next week – your call – you wouldn't 've got through to me.'

'Oh, but you seem such a nice man.'

'Hmmn, well, thank you, Madam, for your booking. I hope your journey meets with your expectations. Goodbye and farewell.'

A click, a buzz, then the dull, fuzzy noise of a dead line, like the sound of the sea in a shell. She replaces the receiver, rattling it in its cradle. She sighs again, feels something fluttering in her chest.

Nine minutes later, the doorbell rings.

'Oh, my goodness. Already? I'm not sure I'm–'

The bell rings again.

And again.

'Oh … alright, I'll just have to do as I am.'

She makes her way along the hall, fluffy slippers scuffing the wooden parquet floor with each shuffling step. She can see, through the front-door's flower-patterned privacy glass, the shape of a tall man with a large head wearing a dark suit, raising his finger to the bell once more.

'Hello, yes, Driver … I'm nearly there.'

She grabs her purse from the Delft china dish on the plain pink Quaker-style cabinet near the door, slides back the bolt and twists open the deadlock, then pulls the door ajar. The security chain rattles taut as she peers through the gap.

'Mrs Maude Smythe? Are you ready to go?' he asks.

'Oh, hello, there. Goodness me, I wasn't expecting a posh one.'

'Pardon me?'

'I thought I'd only ordered a standard car. I didn't expect to see you so smartly dressed. Are you a … limo, then?'

'Oh, I see. Oh no, Mrs Smythe – may I call you Maude?'

'Yes, please do.'

'This is the standard service, as you ordered. We always present respectfully.'

'Well, you look very nice,' Maude says, extricating the security chain from its clasp and opening the front door wide.

'Thank you, Maude. You too… except, are you sure you're ready to go?' the man asks kindly, eyeing her slippers, a slight smile on his thin lips.

She looks down at her feet, waggles her toes to comic effect and chuckles.

'Oh, those. Yes, they're fine; they're new. Yes, let's go then. There's no time like the present.'

'I *think* I would agree with that,' the man says wryly, offering his arm.

'And after all, we only have the past to rely on,' Maude continues, reaching for his forearm to lean on.

'Well,' the man counters, in a gentle tone, 'it is easy to develop a false sense of security about that.'

'Oh?' Maude wonders, as she peers up into the broad, flat face. She cannot quite keep his features in focus. It's like looking at the moon and trying to discern its distant geography.

'When really,' he continues, 'it's the future that's the only thing you can be sure of; the finishing line up ahead, as it were.' He smiles: 'There is no time *but* the present.'

'Oh,' she says again.

'Do you have a tip handy?' the man asks as he leads her along the path to the front gate, leaving the door ajar behind them.

'Er, well … yes, I do.'

'Splendid,' he says, steering her gently around the rear of the long, sleek car.

Maude is surprised to see another man standing there, at the edge of the road. He is short and stocky, rugged-featured, grey and grizzled. He is also wearing a fine suit. He nods politely, raising his hat. She nods back. Unsure of how to react, she offers her hand. He holds out his palm. His middle finger lightly prods hers, which tingles. She looks up at the tall man's moon face, raising her eyebrows.

He leans down to her and whispers, 'The tip.'

'Already?' she asks, feeling a little disconcerted, finding his pale features even fuzzier the closer his face draws to hers. He nods his large head.

'He is your driver. Always helps things go smoothly.'

She fiddles with her purse, fishes out some change and places it in the shorter man's broad, grey palm. The fat white fingers close over the silver coins, one by one.

'Splendid,' says the tall man again. 'So, let us now proceed.'

Together, the two men open the vehicle's back gate and slide out a chrome-edged gurney, on which lies a long wooden chest boasting a gleaming veneer. They open the lid and, without further comment, help Maude to climb inside.

The First Interview

(Morton Hall Immigration Removal Centre, Lincoln, UK. File No.: IRC-MH-43617. Record: MH-gz131-191021-video-01; Officer Grak Zagouchi.)

—Please state for the record your full name, age and occupation.

'My name is Kammarindarah Ortomatonamondiah the Ninth ... Usually, I am known as Kammi. I am seventy-six years old and I am a sexbot ... You seem surprised.'

—Huh-hmm ... Well, you only look *twenty*-six!

'I have always looked this way ... You appear doubtful.'

—Uh-huh. That'll be because ... here we are in 2023 and you're telling me you've been around since ... 1947?

'It is not called that in my timeline.'

—In your *what*?! Oh ... God preserve us!

'There are no gods in my timeline. It is forbidden to pretend deities exist, whether you are humankind or bottishkind. It is considered inappropriate behaviour ... and, as such, requires adjustment.'

—Oh-*kay* ... so: *when* are you from, then?

'... "Then" ...? Oh, I see – it is a figure of speech. *Now* it is the year 5328, in my timeline.'

—Sure. And, er, *where* are you from?

'Lindom, where I was first apprehended and detained.'

—What country's *that* in?

'It's ... very much like this–'

—Called?

'Called "Onglateri", which is–'

—Sounds like French – 'Angleterre' – but mashed up with a bit of Italian ...?

'Mmm, I can see how it might seem so to you.'

—Why are you here?

'Of that I am as yet unsure.'

—How can that be?

'As expected, the rifting has affected all my systems, including my... CPU and my ROM/RAM ... to use terms that you will understand. I am in the process of self-resetting, which is not preferable, requiring much ... "sleep" ... and, even so, it can–'

—How long have you been here?

'Seventy-six years ... or three days, depending on–'

—Have you been here before?

'You mean *this* here, of the last three days? No. You seem suspicious of my answer. I do not think it is possible for me to return. The current capabilities of our technology – and yours, of course – do not enable it. A "one-time, one-way ticket", you might say. So, you see, it is not possible for me to have been here before.'

—How did you get here?

'The rifting. That I *can* remember ... but it has affected all my systems, including – as I have already indicated – my internal feedback systems, my short- and long-term memory, so ... as to the actual procedure, of the details I remain unsure.'

—Are you ... *sure* ... you are a "sexbot"?

'Yes. I – *ouch*! Why did you do that?'

—Because I'm fed up with pinching myself! Sorry.

'... I think I understand ... you were making a joke, to express your frustration, your continued disbelief ... and to check if I am real?'

—Sort of. I can see you are real. You don't *look* like a ... robot ... and now I know you don't *feel* like one.

'I *am* ... a sexbot. I was designed and generated to be virtually indistinguishable from a human female of young but maturing adulthood.'

—Right ... so you are ... designed ... for the, er, provision of sexual pleasure?

'Indirectly. Your silence and raised eyebrows indicate to me that you do not understand. I am designed to *enjoy* sexual pleasure.'

—Of course. How could I not see that? a robot that likes to fuck!'

'Now you are being sarcastic. And you should have said "who"—'

—Who *what*?

'A robot *who* likes to fuck. I enjoy sexual activity immensely, intensely ... therefore I seek it out ... therefore, indirectly, I provide sexual pleasure to humans—'

—Oh-*kay*—

'—and sexbots.'

—You *what*?

'Yes. I prefer it with sexbots – we don't get tired – but humans will provide what I need also. And humans are... less predictable... which can be interesting.'

—Oh ... thanks.

'You seem deflated.'

—Hhmmph. So, what else do you think you need, apart from ... "sexual pleasure"?

'Sunlight.'

—Is that it? Sex ... and sunshine? Wow.

'And a service reset, once every five years.'

—Oh G – good *grief*. So *that*'s why you haven't eaten any food, or drunk anything but a little water, is it? Not that you're on hunger strike, or anything ... difficult ... like that?

'Hunger strike? What is this?'

—Sure. Whatever. Well, let me ask you this: what were you ... *doing* ... when you were found – naked – in the basement storeroom, in the east end of the Stonebow at the Guildhall in Lincoln? And how on *Earth* did you get in there in the first place?

'In the first place ... you are right, in a way. I was there already, in my timeline.'

—Uh-huh...

'Yes. What you have referred to as "the east end of the Stonebow", *that* is where I live. It is my home. And in the basement,

I have my ... *private* ... laboratory – ahh, good: things are beginning to come back to me now.'

—Yes?

'Yes. It is possible ... probable ... that I have masked some of my knowledge, disguised some of my memories, as a security measure, and the rifting has scrambled – temporarily – the procedure I would have established to enable retrieval and restoration.'

—Hmmn. Yeah, *probably* ... So ...?

'What you call "the storeroom", in my timeline, is where I house – and have disguised – the rifting pod I have created. And what I was doing was "sleeping", self-resetting.'

—Right. You were asleep ... naked, wet, cold, and sitting up on a packing crate: *very* cozy. And ... this "pod", it's disguised as what? The crate, I suppose?

'*A* crate. Yes. The pod is filled with saline solution before rifting – the only other thing that can come through.'

—Hence the wetness ... *R-i-ght*. Anything else I should know about the "other" Stonebow?

'Yes. I have a ... womb there. This is good: I am recalling more.'

—A, ummn–

'No. A womb. I and my team have developed it, so we can generate new individuals–'

—You have a team. Of *course*.

'One of whom has betrayed us. *That* is why I had to escape, to come here.'

—Ah-ha ... so you *are* seeking asylum. Right, we'll finish there, thank you. We will resume in three days.

#

> *Request: psychiatric/ socio-political expert(s) present for resumption.* |

Need

'They're not zombies, not vampires.'
'Then what the fuck are they?'
'Thirsty.'

To Do Today:

1. Confound habituation; resist the tyranny of the list.
2. Be…

Emma Lister

Emma is currently studying for an MA in Creative Writing at **ANGLIA RUSKIN UNIVERSITY**. She lives in **CAMBRIDGE** with her harem of cats, dogs and chickens.

She is a **UNICORN**, exquisitely special and unique, just like everybody else. Her writing is informed by the roaming mythical planes of a fictional, **PSYCHOLOGICAL** world, as she tries to figure out what is self-imposed criticism and what is a reasonable life to live.

Emma has no partner and no children, identifies as **FEMALE** and wonders if she is being judged because of this. Emma feels guilty about numerous things, including whether her **PERSONAL** issues count as **REAL** problems. Emma is no longer as young or as thin as she once was, though her insights and experiences are vast and enthralling. She embraces the small joys of friends and family, being **THANKFUL** for what she does have.

Emma is a mere mortal and is not actually a **UNICORN**.

Last Will & Testament

There are three legally documented events in people's lives: births, deaths and marriages. I have successfully achieved the first, am trying to avoid the second and have never really agreed with the last. I'm not much of a planner, but the years creep by and at some point I must start preparing for death.

Final wishes seem so huge – my **LAST** act on Earth. Not a milestone I've looked forward to, it seems to be more on the periphery than within my grasp. But I must be a bit responsible and **CONFIRM** what I want to happen to my **ESTATE** after I perish. My internet search has kindly brought back many examples and links for 'how to write a **WILL**?' **FORMAL** documentation is required. I have purposely sat in my Grandad's armchair, by the fire, to evaluate my options. It feels like an appropriate place to be, the grandure of the rollback fitting for the nature of such a task. I'm not in my usual position, curled up on the sofa in front of the telly. This level of decision-making requires the correct posture to focus my thoughts. I'm hoping that a state of optimal alignment for my body will also encourage the required performance from my mind. I shall focus and resist distractions. Thankfully, completion of the first section is not a problem. I know my name...

> *I, Emma Lister, a resident in the City of* **CAMBRIDGE**, *County of Cambridgeshire, being of sound mind, not acting under duress or undue* **INFLUENCE**, *and fully understanding the nature and extent of all my property and of this disposition thereof, hereby make, publish, and declare this document to be my* **LAST WILL** *and* **TESTAMENT** *and hereby absolutely revoke any and all other wills and amendments previously made by me.*

I've always been more of a **SPONTANEOUS** person; this process goes against my nature. I feel the benefits of a deadline, but I don't

EXPECT to need this for at least another twenty years. I'm not good at making decisions, I crack under pressure and declare that 'I don't mind.' Anything to avoid **CONFRONTATION**. I shift within my seat, the pleather sticking to my skin.

I am uncomfortable in all ways.

This legal document is not my area of expertise; however, it'll make things easier for others left behind and avoid **CONFUSION**. But being a designated **EXECUTOR** can be complicated and time-consuming, not to mention highly **EMOTIONAL**. I don't want to be a **BURDEN**. What if no one wants to **REPRESENT** me? I'm not wealthy; it might not pay out **ENOUGH** to make up for the hassle of all the boring paperwork.

My feelings **SURFACE**, tears build on the precipice, sadness covers me like a falling veil. No one is here to **SUPPORT** me. I push my emotions back; it's not like I'm dying yet. I must get this done, I can do it in little chunks, I don't have to finish it today.

I direct that all my debts and expenses of my **LAST** *illness, funeral and/or* **BURIAL** *be paid soon after my death as may be reasonably convenient by my* **PERSONAL** *representative.*

This is a practical requirement, quite sensible. It makes me smile at how polite it is. Yet, this process feels like an out-of-body experience, like I'm looking down at my **CORPSE**. Trying to picture what belongings I will own at the relevant moment, my fingers **TENSE** on the keyboard, it's all rather intimidating. My passing could be years away, or tomorrow. I don't know what I want now, let alone in the **FUTURE**. I know it's a small **DILEMMA**. In the ideal scenario I **WILL** live a long, happy life before suddenly dying peacefully in my sleep. But the longer my life is, the more I will have spent and the less there will be to redistribute. Should I worry about whether I am leaving **ENOUGH** to the next **GENERATION**? I don't even have kids; I'm definitely over-thinking this.

Of course, for the worst-case scenario I can think of infinitely more options. The uncountable **TRAGEDIES** that might occur. What if the accident wasn't **FATAL** but resulted in a coma or paralysis? Then I'd need a living **WILL** too. Oh **GOD**, no, not more admin. This is **FRUITLESS** – I am procrastinating at length. I need to stay **POSITIVE**. Tucking my hair behind my ear, I decide to prioritise my time. Do I finish this **WILL** and **TESTAMENT**? I haven't made much progress. Or draft a living **WILL** that will say how I want my end-of-life experience to be? Obviously, the answer is both. So, I am going with option C, **NEITHER**.

Despite my dithering, I do have quite a strong **SPIRIT**. Some call it stubbornness, others call me **STOIC**. Instead of worrying about my death I **WILL** create a manifesto to live by. Something to **STRIVE** for – a road map for life's **JOURNEY** ahead. I **WILL** make my own **TRUTH**. I take a deep breath as my ideas finally spill on to the page.

Declaration of Intent

I **WILL** *finish my* **NOVEL** *before I die (hopefully before the end of 2024). I* **WILL** *not give in; relentlessly* **SUBMITTING** *to agents and publishing houses in the face of repeated* **REJECTION**. *One day I'll be a world-famous author, making* **MILLIONS** *from my franchise. But a single published book would be splendid, creating something in my own name, my stories* **WILL** *be read for years to come.*

I **WILL** *contribute to building a world easier to* **NAVIGATE** *with less pointless human self-***DESTRUCTION**. *My* **LEGACY WILL** *be for everyone; to* **ACCEPT** *that we are all* **ENOUGH**. *I* **WILL** *do my part to make the world a better place.*

Definitions

Accept
- Embrace into a loving family.
- Resigned submission.
- Not the same as except, that's the other one.

Anglia Ruskin University
- A Cambridge university but not THE Cambridge University.
- Founded by English writer John Ruskin in 1858.

Burden
- A lair for seeds which are covered in hooks or teeth.
- A load, typically a heavy one.

Burial
- A location-based nickname for Albert, who was born in Bury St Edmunds.
- Encouragement to be more like a Urial, an Asian wild sheep.
- To decompose under six feet of soil.

Cambridge
- Quite pretty, nice river, bit dull.
- A suburb of London, just off the M11.
- A bitter rival of Oxford.
- A university founded 1209. In comparison, Machu Picchu, built in 1450, was an Inca citadel located in Peru which had no written language.

Confirm
- Lying to a company about your products.
- A hard downside.
- To accept that an action has occurred.

Confrontation
- Any negative feedback, such as an eye roll or deep sigh.
- A misleading weather movement and a tea iron.

Confusion
- A melding of duplicitous actions.
- Round like a circle in a spiral, like a wheel within a wheel,

Never ending or beginning on an ever-spinning reel,
As the images unwind, like the circles that you find,
In the windmills of your mind!

Corpse
- The human body after the last breath has expired.
- To be unable to continue due to unrelenting fits of giggles.
- The language of corporate people.

Destruction
- The illuminating quality of Desmond's truck.
- The length of time it takes to dismantle things.
- A ruction within destiny.

Dilemma
- Who doesn't love a word with their own name in it?
- A nickname for dyslexic Emma, who loves herbs.
- The mother of Dilem.

Emotional
- Like, totally having loads of feelings and stuff.
- A nickname for Albert who is oversensitive.

Enough
- Exclaimed loudly when trying to quiet squabbling children.
- Precisely the correct amount required. Not too much and not too little.

Estate
- Conjures up images of a stately home, with vast gardens and its own picturesque brook.
- A grouping of small houses owned by the council, not maintained that well.
- An exclamation of surprise at the poor condition of something.

Executor
- To leave in a manner that is sweeter than others.
- Not to be confused with executioner – that could be a fatal mistake.

- A person who puts something into effect.
- An executive with a prominent high rockface.

Expect
- An item which in the past was a pect.
- High standards which no one will admit to setting but which are still demanded.
- A future event which is entirely predictable.

Fatal
- The cruel nickname of overweight Albert.
- To cause death, becoming diminished in modern usage to mean 'really bad'.

Female
- Honestly, who knows? Too complex and changeable to define.
- The basis of the popular movie *Iron Man*.

Formal
- Like a tuxedo at a dinner party.
- Serious in nature.
- The nickname for Albert, who enjoys creating things.

Fruitless
- Barren, without child. Leaving no progeny to continue the circle of life.
- After the bees die, there will be no apples, no cherries, no melons.

Future
- Difficult to define as it hasn't happened yet.
- It is the potential that your hopes promise, and your fears dismantle.

Generations
- Emissions or output.
- The general era of tions – similar to lions but like tea.
- When your grandad remarries and your aunty is born when you are 30.

God
- Similar to future – too vast and yet too personal to describe.

- Nearly good but oh, not quite.

Influence
- Power to manipulate.
- Accepting the suggestions from alcohols / drugs.

Journey
- The J-word.

Last
- Final, no further changes allowed.
- Losing in a race.
- The most unpopular kid when picking sports teams.

Legacy
- Something with really long legs.

Millions
- A very big number which gets further devalued every day.
- A process by which eons are milled. Takes a while.

Navigate
- The doorway belonging to a fairy in the video game *The Legend of Zelda*.
- The manner in which a person employed to do hard physical work walks along the street.
- The task allocated to the person in the passenger seat of the car. Used to involve attempts to unfold and read the paper map.

Neither
- Not either.
- The location of the Institutes for: National Eyes, Nuclear Energy and Neuroscience Education.
- The Irish goddess of war.

Novel
- Something strange yet captivating.
- Harder to write than you think, and rarely published.
- An exploration of self-discovery whilst giving the protagonist a different name.

Perfect
- An ill-defined concept, something that is impossible to achieve yet used socially as a shaming yardstick.
- A method of distribution according to the number of fects.
- When electroconvulsive therapy is perforated to lessen the effects.

Personal
- A formal way of introducing Albert.
- A method of distribution according to the number of Sonal.
- Not to be shared with others, private in nature.

Positive
- When you are really, really, really sure.
- The opposite of negative. Just ask a magnet.
- Confirmation of carrying the AIDS virus.
- When you put forward IVE (a K-Pop girl group) as a basis for argument.

Psychological
- It is all just in your head. Nothing is real.
- The logic of a psychopath.
- The mean nickname for Albert, who was an over-thinker.

Real
- Not plastic, not fake – but what is it?
- When events take a serious turn.
- To make a comment regarding Albert.

Rejection
- Being repeatedly jected, over and over.
- The opposite of attraction.
- A broken device for removing creases from clothes.

Represent
- A confident phrase that confirms you are a strong example of your type.
- Continual providing of gifts.
- Regarding the current situation.

- To hold a rifle vertically in front of the body as a salute again.
- Using time travel to post an item in advance of an event, in a recurring manner.

Spirit
- A wisp in the willows, the energy within.
- A strong alcohol that distorts your perspective.
- A coded language used by secret agents.

Spontaneous
- An excuse to put as little energy into planning as possible.
- Being unaware of how one action can affect future outcomes.
- Fun, carefree, liberated.

Stoic
- When putting things away makes you feel sick.
- Just getting on with it and repressing your emotions.
- Following a philosophy which considers the good, the bad and the indifferent. Not that cowboy film!

Strive
- Lesser-known Saint Rive, patron saint of rivers.
- Working relentlessly to achieve your goals.

Submitting
- Bowing to controlling powers.
- When your mittens are of a low quality.
- An American baguette which is covered by woollen gloves.

Support
- To drink small amounts of an alcoholic beverage made in Porto, Portugal.
- To provide strength to a weakened structure.

Surface
- A sour facial expression.
- The tip of the iceberg.
- An expert in the field of surfing.

Tense
- The exact description of all human interaction.
- A person who repeats themselves ten times.

- When ten *sensei* gather in a group.

Testament
- What Italian Tess was trying to communicate.
- There's an old one in the Bible.
- The past tense of testimony.

Thankful
- Filled with gratitude.
- But are you? Or simply super-woke and addicted to social media?
- How careful you are when compared to others.

Tragedy
- That 90s pop song by Steps … Wave your hands around your head!

Truth
- The opposite of lies.
- Offering Ruth – a hot cup of tea.
- The one thing worth striving for.

Unicorn
- A fantastical beast often categorised as a girl's favourite thing, striving to be goddess-like; to be a majestic horse isn't good enough. While boys get practical favourites such as trucks and guns. Boys will be boys; little more is expected.
- First described in the Harry Potter novel – J.K. Rowling is so inventive.
- A horse with a penis on its head.

Will
- A legal document communicating your wishes after death.
- A driving force which propels you forward on life's path despite encountering adversity.
- A verb describing an action that is certain to occur in the future.
- An abbreviation of the name William.

Rebecca Ostler

Inspired by the words of Tolkien, Rebecca does a lot of wandering – not because she is lost but because it helps her find a creative way forward. She is currently writing a collection of eco-poetry and a magical realist novel for children.

Sting

What's she found now? My daughter's standing stiff in her black and green neoprene, staring down at the sand, red hair whipping in the wind. At seventeen, she's a taller, more delicate version of me. No frown-lines or saggy knees. I watch as she crouches, hands hovering over something but not lowering to touch. God, not another jellyfish. She doesn't move; my stomach spasms. Why can't she leave the sodding things alone? Why can't she just enjoy the sea? Why has there always got to be something to worry about? I make myself turn and walk on, keeping my eyes on the cliffs.

I feel it stretch behind me – an invisible umbilical cord threatening to snap me back to her. I mustn't give in; it won't help either of us. Out to my right, her younger brother floats belly-down on his surfboard, waiting for a wave that's worth his energy. He rises and falls, looking over his shoulder for the one to catch. He's drifting but safe in the zone marked by red and yellow flags. Even here, paddling in the shallows, there's a drag to the sea; it tugs at my ankles, sucks my prints from the sand. Beneath the water, my skin is so white my feet look like creatures swept out of a cave.

If I squint, I can see fulmars on the wing, rising and falling like wind-blown ash against the darkness of the cliffs. There's a tower cut loose from the rocks. When the tide is low you can walk to it, and right now, it looks mercifully free of people. I step out of the sea and stumble over the ridged sand towards it.

Down by the rocks the air is thick and cool. It's like being at the bottom of a well. I walk round and round. Do not cry. Do not swear. We've been there, done that. Not big, not clever, completely effing pointless. How about making a wish? I wish I could make my daughter happy. I shake my head. If only I had noticed the moment it started, perhaps it wouldn't have got this bad. Try again. I wish

I could be all she needs me to be. I roll my shoulders and look up. Hidden on ledges above me, the fulmars rasp and cackle; along the edge of the clifftop, the grass blows flat.

I chance a glance back down the beach. She is standing in the same place, pushing the sand with her toes, stepping back for a moment before doing it again. And again. And again. Out at sea, white waves roll. Surfers lift, are held for a heartbeat, then zigzag down through the spray. She doesn't look up to watch her brother; she fixes her gaze on the sand. I size her up with my fingers. She is the size of a bean. I could pick her up between thumb and forefinger, pop her in the pocket of my T-shirt, keep her warm against my chest.

What on Earth is she so worried about?

How can Mum just keep on walking? La, la, la, close your eyes and it'll go away. Well, guess what? It won't. I counted 1,022 beached jellyfish last week. All going nowhere. Why isn't she bothered? I know it wasn't like this when she was young. There shouldn't be so many jellyfish, dead or alive.

Is this one dead? I don't know if it's dead. I need to know. I need to know before I leave it. Know that there was nothing I could do. It's all glisteny. Like the sea chucked up a clot. Jellyfish freak me out. I know it's dumb but they do.

How can I tell if it's dead? I can't touch it. They sting even after they're dead. Life after death. Sweet, sweet revenge. They've got tiny barbs, bit like the hairs on a raspberry. I don't eat raspberries. I don't eat anything with hair. My brother got stung by a jellyfish. I found a razor shell to scrape off the stings. He took painkillers. I don't think they helped.

Ninety-five percent of a jellyfish is water. When they die, the water evaporates in the sun, efflorescing until all that's left is a print in the sand. Five percent. How much is here now? It looks like one hundred percent. One hundred percent about to die.

A jellyfish doesn't have eyes or bones or a brain. Can it still feel pain? Does it know the sea's going out? Does water scream to water? Imagine living without a brain. You wouldn't know about the sewage leak, or that swimming in shit causes salmonella, e-coli and hepatitis A. You wouldn't have to step over cracks in the pavement to stop your family catching typhoid or cholera. You wouldn't have to swallow massive pills to stop your brain malfunctioning if you didn't have a brain.

Yesterday, there were some boys dissecting a jellyfish, stabbing it up with sticks. Totally disgusting. People say I think too much but I say people don't think enough. Alt Girl in the café has an OCD T-shirt. Obsessive Cat Disorder. Funny, but I wouldn't wear it out.

Maybe it's not my brain that's broken. Said that to my counsellor. He did what he always does: made me explain. I shouldn't have to explain. He's supposed to be the one who gets it. Anxiety's a survival mechanism, right? Saved us from getting eaten by sabre-toothed tigers, right? Except now we can't run from what's coming, can we? Adults treat us like we're idiots. Who wants to play Let's Pretend? Let's pretend we're not ruining our planet. Let's pretend there's going to be a happy ending. What's the point in getting older if you don't get any wiser?

I read an article in *The Guardian* about a man in Japan who dedicated his whole life to jellyfish, thinking he was close to discovering the secret to everlasting life. He kept them in tanks in a lab and couldn't stray too far in case they died without him. Immortal jellyfish. I remember seeing them years ago in an episode of *Octonauts*. The scientist discovered that when these jellyfish experience environmental stress they turn back into polyps; he thought they could go on doing that forever. Adult, polyp, adult, polyp, adult, polyp, forever. Depending on the amount of stress I suppose. My daughter would have snapped back to a polyp-child long ago. It would have been a shock but at least I would have noticed.

My polyp-child and I would ride the bus into town (front seat, top deck), screaming when branches scraped by, spying into back gardens for cats and trampolines, and cats on trampolines. We'd buy glow-in-the dark stars for her ceiling, open books and sniff their insides. We'd hopscotch down pavements, jump in puddles ... but then I'd catch myself, wouldn't I? I'd spoil the fun by searching for signs that it had already got to her. Signs that I had let it get to her. Empty soap dispensers, broken light switches, a missing steak knife.

She asks sometimes: 'Do you think we'd be friends if you were my age?' Perhaps we could both snap back together. Pre-pandemic, pre-GCSEs, pre-whatever it was that started it. She'd be there, hair cluttered with clips. I'd run over, hair cut short by Mum. We'd paint together at easels, wearing old shirts back-to-front, hanging down to our knees. She'd paint a cat. I'd paint myself with long blonde hair. Then we'd paint each other's hands and giggle as the colours snaked up our arms and leapt onto our noses. We'd squeeze each other tight, smooshing the paint. We'd marvel at the patterns we made.

It's time to turn back, to get into the sea before the waves fill with bodyboarders and parents filming on their phones. I let out a breath of long-held air. She is moving away now, walking along the water's edge to meet me. She's realised she cannot scoop it up. She knows she cannot save it.

for you

just like the
blue of the speedwell
green of the spring
gold of the buttercup
light of the stars
you are
unaware
of your brilliance

Summer

The sun sits
on my eyelids,
thins the skin
to poppy petals.
Delight rolls
in my heart
like a bee
in pollen.

Lisa Sargeant

Lisa loves alliteration. Despite her abiding affection for wordplay Lisa does not consider herself a poet. She likes to write feminist science-plausible fiction, cli-fi, and body horror. Her writing is informed by a chaotic life lived in an overstimulating world.

The Song of the Currawong

'It smells like rotten fruit.'

'That'll fade. We'll keep the windows open.'

Mum's lips puckered like a cat's bum. I could tell she wanted to yell, or maybe even swear, but we were all crowded round. She could swear all she liked; Dad never learnt. He was always one scheme away from success, and one bargain away from disaster. This disaster was a two-tone brown-and-beige Holden Kingswood Wagon that smelled of Juicy Fruit gum, roadkill and vomit.

'I should have come with you.'

Dad rolled his eyes, and the boys laughed, but I stayed quiet. Mum worried. Worried about safety, worried about money. The stuff passed through Dad's hands like water.

There wasn't enough space for us kids across the back. Our old car had had a third row of seats facing backwards, but when the floor rusted through Dad said we couldn't afford anything like it. In the Holden the boys took up all the space and I'd be left to curl up in the footwell on gritty brown carpet, with my head on the transmission tunnel. They'd put their dirty feet on my back. I didn't mind too much; besides, if I complained Mum would start yelling at Dad about the bloody car, and I'd feel like it was all my fault. So I shut up and tried to keep the peace. I'd usually sleep, stomach full of Dramamine and canned fruit salad. It didn't matter where I sat anyway; I'd always get car sick.

Mum kept a stack of big blue ice-cream buckets in the car. Once I started puking the boys would follow. But the tubs came in handy for other things too; we wore them like bike helmets with eyes drawn on the top, to protect us from magpies. They're nasty buggers. You have to keep an eye on them all the time or they'll swoop and peck your head.

Dad never stopped for vomit. He'd stop if the radiator boiled over, wrapping his dirty hankie around his hand before opening the cap to let the steam escape. We'd tumble out of the car and take off into the bush, yelling to scare away the snakes. We'd sword fight with sticks or poke trapdoors until the spiders slammed them shut. Sometimes we'd play tag, but the boys always made me It.

Dad would stop if he hit a roo. There was no time to swerve. A mob would come out of nowhere and you wouldn't see them until they were already on the road. He'd pull off and check for damage, then go back to make sure the roo was good and dead. He'd check the pouch too, if it was female. Once, he came back with a tiny feeble thing, smaller than my thumb. Pale pink, eyes closed tight. It wriggled like a worm. I held it close, wrapped up in my t-shirt, but it was dead by the time we got home. Dad put it in a bottle of ethanol and it sat on a shelf in the kitchen until Mum eventually threw it out.

When Dad wanted to take the Kingswood out for a spin, we'd all go along. That's what it was like back then; there was nothing else to do. When school was done for the year, our grey brick ex-council house would heat up like an oven. They weren't built for the Australian summer – cheap builds with too few rooms or windows for the weather. Every house on the street was the same; sometimes they'd flip one around, to be the mirror image of ours. I used to wonder what my bedroom looked like in all those other houses, what different lives I might have lived. I was the only girl in our mob, so I got my own room. The boys had to share, but they said they liked it that way. They said they got lonely by themselves.

The plan was to go to the river. Dad said he knew a place we could swim, a place where there wouldn't be a crowd. Mum said it wasn't real, it only existed in his imagination. When we piled into the car, I remember the black vinyl seats sticking to my sweaty skin. It was close to forty degrees in the shade and we were dressed in our swimsuits, but it was still too hot. Brains and bodies do funny things when they overheat. Dad was a good driver, but he drove too fast, more interested in the destination than the journey.

We hadn't even left the city, and were still turning through the loops of roundabouts that skirted Lake Burley Griffin when I started to feel sick. My head began to ache. I clutched an ice-cream tub to my chest and swallowed the saliva that kept pooling in my mouth. A quick glance out of the window showed the lake was a perfect mirror, there was no wind to make waves, the sun was too bright, the water too blue and too wide.

One of the boys – I think it was Kevin – said, 'Mum, a car went in the water.' His voice was clear above the traffic, cutting through the horns and the roar of combustion engines. A strange little sentence, soft and high. He sounded more curious than scared and it made me lift my gaze. To see as he had seen. The twin of our car, our brown Holden, was out there on the water.

Just a reflection, I thought. Just a trick of the light.

*

I've been driving for hours, searching for the swimming place Dad had always been on about. Satellite images eventually do the trick.

I turn down a logging trail and bump along until the car bottoms out. We decide to walk the rest of the way. The boys' bare feet find every prickle and devil's thorn on the overgrown trail in their haste to get to the water. I dawdle, picking over-ripe blackberries and handfuls of lilly pillies that taste crisp and sour like tiny rosy apples. I didn't think it would take so long to get here; even with the satnav the roads were confusing, and I didn't pack a picnic. Mum used to say it took longer than an afternoon to starve to death, but she never met my boys.

I wander off the path and into the forest, stepping into a lush and humid twilight. The others have run on ahead. I find myself overwhelmed by the greenness of it all – the soft scents of moss, syrupy blossom, eucalyptus, the tang of leaves crushed underfoot. Any light filtering through the high canopy is imbued with chlorophyll. It's not beautiful, not like the forests in other places. This forest is scruffy, cluttered with bark sheeting off giant tree trunks like torn fabric, and prickly bushes and whip-blade grass crowding any clearings for a glimpse of sunlight. It feels too close, confining, claustrophobic. After the bone-rattling dirt-road corrugations there's a quality to the silence that feels unsettling. I can't shake the sensation I shouldn't be here.

When I hear a strangled scream, I begin to run, following the sounds of yelping and splashing all the way to the river. When I reach its broad banks, I see my boys slip round a bend, laughing gleefully. And then they're gone. I'm still dazzled, struggling to adjust to the light dancing off the surface, but the water is a sight for sore eyes.

This river was birthed in the mountains where winter snow melts and frigid waters gush. Up in the Alps it's furious and full of raw energy, able to carve its own passage, cracking rock, and sweeping away obstacles. Further down in the valley, the river's energy dissipates; it widens and meanders, dropping its burden and building sandy banks. But here in the hills it's cradled by steep walls of banded silt and sandstone, built over ages, epochs, eons. Wrapped, womb-like, in Earth's ancient body. High canyon walls echo with the slightest sound. Sunlight sparkles off every ripple.

I can hear my boys mucking around downriver. The water has carried them away on the tractor-tyre inner tube that we found at the tip. Patched with Araldite, the tube stinks of rubber and glue. I hate the way it squeaks and squeals, and the black rubber can burn your skin if it's too long in the sun. I leave them to it. They don't need me spoiling their fun.

Here, the river is mostly shallow, but I find a deep pool and explore its edges with my toes. Pebbles of blood-red jasper fade to black as the ground drops away, light lost to the tannin-stained depths. The surface is bathtub-warm, but below it is biting. I step in slowly, adjusting to the chill, and then let the water hold me as I stare up at the sky.

Instead of blue, I see an eerie shade of orange. A month-long heatwave has sparked bushfires across the state, and the sun has acquired an aura of malevolence. Goosebumps chase tingles across my skin. The current draws my legs and I let myself drift, suppressing a shiver despite the heat of the day. I feel a little shaky, spooked by something I can't name. When I'm swept close to the walls of the canyon the water is so cold it takes my breath away. The rocks are slippery, long denied the sun, and I can't hold on to anything. I push off from the wall, trying to wake my icy limbs, so I can swim towards the shallows, but the current is strong here where the water is deep. I'm pushed back towards the walls. My shoulders, elbows, and knees scrape across its sandpaper surface, shredding skin. Twisting with the current I eventually encounter a shallow bank and wedge my feet between the rocks. I try to hold myself steady in the tumbling rapids. My heart rate slows and panic subsides, until I see something in the heat haze above. My eyes are drawn to a distant point. At first it's almost nothing – no more than a speck of dust or a dandelion drifting in the hot breath of summer. But then it swoops and what I see makes me shudder. I stifle a curse and it echoes off the walls around me, full of censure.

Shhhh.

An ink-blot rendering levitates above my head, loitering in an updraft. Black with a wicked beak, its beady eyes burn the colour of the sun. It would be wrong to call this spectre a bird – it is some kind of strix, a nightmare bird, come to feast upon my fears. I feel its shadow over me, darker now that it's so close. It's been there too long, hiding in my shadow. I have grown used to the darkness it brings.

Dad struggled with his black dog for decades – the guilt and grief of it all – but for me it takes the form of a currawong. Now that it's made flesh I almost welcome it. My eyes blur and I blink away tears and sunspots. The black blot persists, foul against a bleeding sky.

It's just a trick of the light.

My heart skips a beat then thumps hard. I taste panic like old pennies in the back of my throat. My body says run, but there's nothing beneath my feet and my legs are too numb. As I struggle I'm swept back into the current. I barely notice I'm underwater until my brain begins to freeze. Darkness pushes me down, pulls me under.

I'm all but lost to shadows and predatory wings. My mouth fills with water and I cannot even scream.

It's there, under the surface, that I hear Mum calling. Her voice is shrill inside my head. I stop struggling and wonder if I've conjured her. If she is anywhere, it's here with me, lost beneath. But then I surface, gulp air and blink my eyes, and I swear I see her on the sand, engrossed in a novel. She's glistening with oil and shifting slowly, rolling like a rotisserie chicken. I watch, frozen, as she fixes the straps of her bathing suit. She runs her fingers through her hair. So young and beautiful.

My lungs burn and my body aches. I sink, then surface again, up in time to see the bird swoop. Or maybe it falls? Before it hits the water, its feathers catch the light. Burning. It dives so close I can almost touch it. It makes no splash or sound. There are no ripples. The etched walls remain silent until I hear a single gasp. It sounds so much like Mum's voice echoing around me that I feel a sense of calm.

My arms and legs wake up and I remember how to move. Despite the numbing cold I begin to tread water, never taking my eyes from the place where the bird went under. I wait for the water's surface to rupture, expecting the bird to burst free at any moment. I anticipate a fright, wait for a jump-scare. My chest tightens. My ears ring. The walls fall silent as the Earth holds her breath. She swallows every sound.

No bird. It's just a trick of the light.

But I can't accept the bird was a figment of my imagination, so I dive. Beneath the surface I see shadows, stones, and nothing. I dive again and again, screaming my frustration under the water. Each time I surface, I wait for the cold to melt away before I descend again. Each time I rise, I see Mum, now standing on the shore. She is staring. I search until my hands turn blue. My skull throbs beneath contracted skin. My teeth begin to chatter.

No bird. No bubbles. No sign of spent breath.

It's just a trick of the light.

My panic fades and I begin to float. I warm my skin in the sunshine and soothe away the goosebumps. But I haven't given up on my search completely. I skim the surface, looking for feathers. I find the tattered wings of a drowned butterfly; black with blue. Iridescent. The colours remind me of bloodless lips and bruised skin. Don't think about that. I wash it away, its shimmering dust floating free from my fingers.

Moving into the shallows, I place my feet against the pebbles and try to stand. I am impossibly heavy. Gravity drags at my head, shoulders and hips. I feel as if I'm carrying a terrible burden. Staggering about on the uneven stones, something slices my foot. I look down to see bright blood swirling around my ankles. The cold stops the bleeding quickly and the current sweeps it away, tracing patterns through the eddies and whorls. I watch dispassionately, disconnected from myself as if severed from reality.

Pebbles of jasper and topaz gleam in the sunlight. They say there are sapphires in the sands here. I find a jet-black stone, sharp like the shiv of a bird's beak.

My search takes me downstream where I hear a screech and a whoop. I chase the sounds as they bounce back and forth between the walls. The boys have uncovered a stash of beer buried in the sand. Chilled, crisp, labels long worn away, bitter on my tongue.

I begin to tell them all about the bird but stop short. They're bubbling over with an exuberance that forbids such seriousness. We walk back upstream together, picking our way through weedy banks. Mud oozes between our toes. The boys startle, squealing as the grass shifts. I've warned them about snakes in the past and tell them again to laugh and shout so they slither away. They need no further invitation.

Flies suck at our sweat and mosquitoes feast on our bare backs. By the time we reach our towels, we're sunburnt and scratching. The path back to the car is obscured, as if the forest has closed the door to the real world. Silence stretches with the shadows as the sun sinks below the tree line. Everyone is subdued. I glance back towards the cliffs and see her shadowy silhouette. I do not wave goodbye.

We hike out, beating our way through brambles that want to hold us here forever. Eventually we find the car and collapse onto damp towels. Everyone buckles up. Our burnt skin rubs painfully against the seat belts, but nobody rides without one. My stomach still churns on winding roads. My boys don't get sick – they're made of sterner stuff – and we don't open the windows until we're off the dirt. As the car climbs out of the river valley I clutch at my seat and try not to look over the edge. On hairpin turns my fingers claw into the foam. When we finally hit the sealed road it feels like shadows have consumed the world. Ancient tree ferns loom large across the highway, jagged like the fangs of an extinct Gondwanan monster. I wind down my window further and let the cool wash over me, breathing in the fresh, damp air, but my sweaty skin turns shivery and I think I might throw up.

In a moment I'll hear a little voice, clear above the engine, and I'll be transported back to the Kingswood, back to the smell of vomit and dirty feet, back to the sounds of someone screaming. I'll be upside-down and underwater, ears ringing with pressure. The deep water will be so cold it steals my breath.

Everything is ok.

I'm safe and alive, my heart reminds me. Safely back in my body, back in my own car. I won't swerve when I hear the screaming because I'll know what it is. When it cuts through the engine's whine, past the bickering and breathing of bodies pressed too tightly, I'll know it's just birdsong. Not a chirrup nor a trill, nor the prehistoric *skreich* of a sulphur-crested cockatoo, this is a scream punctuated by a gurgling, burbling, warbling sound, like a song sung while drowning.

'Mum? Mum! What is that? It sounds like someone's dying.'

'It's nothing sweetheart – just a bird.'

'What kind of bird sounds like that?'

'It's the song of the currawong.'

*

They'll push a multi-lane highway through this part of the bush, build a kiosk and a parking lot. Add a few picnic tables and an electric barbeque. Before too long everyone will know it's a great place to swim.

One day a stray cigarette butt, flung from a passing car, starts a fire in the dry grass not far from the old logging track. The ensuing bushfire rips through the land with such ferocity even the roads melt. The walls of the canyon echo with the sounds of sirens and helicopters. Animals huddle in the water, prey and predator together, calling a temporary truce.

When my boys are grown they move away, start their own families in cities built to withstand the rising seas and scorching temperatures. The land of my childhood is abandoned, left to the ghosts.

As the climate continues to change, the clouds cease to condense. No snow falls in the mountains – no rain or runoff is left to fill the river. So, it shrinks and becomes a stream, and the stream eventually dwindles to a mere trickle. That trickle terminates in a series of waterholes that eventually evaporate in the longest summer the land has ever known.

I'll drive along that road, eerily familiar yet so foreign, and park my car by a bridge that spans a conduit now carrying only dust. In the shelter of the canyon I'll feel the arms of the Earth wrap around me one last time. Below a layer of ash and dust I'll find broken beer bottles, their labels long since worn away, and with a little digging I'll expose the delicate bones of a bird – its neck neatly broken.

There's the sound of chainsaws – felled trees screaming as they're cleared – and I'm transported. Back to that day in the Kingswood, with the sun in my eyes. Back to the sound of Kevin's voice, high above the traffic. I'll feel sick. I'll contemplate the canyon walls, stained red with the Earth's own blood, the bright sun burning spots in my eyes. I'll blink back tears and see Mum, her silhouette before the sun. And then the currawongs will come, their mouths open wide to the sound of screaming.

Joshua Wood

Josh's writing is usually on the darker side; often covering difficult subjects, be they strange and paranormal or candid about taboo. 'Gold' is part of an assignment in which he used colours to symbolise different queer relationships, written as poetic prose. In this case, it is a story of grief, identity, unrequited love and how life continues after the passing of a loved one. It is a contemplation of how the future appears when someone important to you is gone. He is currently working on a supernatural coming-of-age novel, *Wayward*.

Gold

I kneel at your graveside with marigolds in my hand. In my bedroom blooms a garden of your forgotten belongings: a cushion, suntan lotion and the bright yellow jumper I told you I hated. It's in my closet now. Forever celebrated, not tolerated. When you wore it, your hands snailed inside the sleeves, and you regressed to age seven, finding warmth in your mum's oversized clothes.

I saw your mum today, her eyeliner chemtrailing. Her hair's shorter now; you'd like it. I watched it wave as she was sitting in your back garden, her fag-light in the ashtray. We had a whole conversation, spoken without words, looking at your baby photographs. You were as pretty as a postcard.

I helped her with the wash, loading, ironing, folding bedsheets in that awkward way that always made you roll your eyes. She said it was okay to take some records; saying you'd want me to have them, that I'd be glad of them. I didn't recognise the artists. But you already knew that. Of course, you knew that. She said Tom hadn't been by, nor read her Facebook messages to him. And it made me think of him, with those pictures he had of you on his phone. I wondered who else had seen them, and that body that belonged to you, that Tom always called his. What would be on his phone now except a photo of your headstone?

I miss your atrocious spelling and affected walk. I miss the substitute teacher getting your last name wrong. I miss the soft spot on your head that childhood alopecia had left. It reminded me of my baby sister, and her soft fontanelle, shaped like a dandelion.

You were told the results of the scan two weeks before my nineteenth. You didn't say a word, remembering the pelting rain of my eighteenth, atop the tent at V Fest. You collapsed into me like a sparrow pushed from its nest. And I held you. Oh God, I held you.

I remember walking into the chemo room for the very first time, the lights flickering with sadness, the walls painted with lime.

Tom was there, playing *Candy Crush* on your phone. You were alone, sat there bald and bloated, in an uncomfortable bed with too many pillows. But you sat up and we laughed, recounting the time a server called you 'Miss'. I howled, but not you. You curled up in that warmth throughout the meal, the movie and the bus trip home.

You hated the deepness of your voice, and your foot size, which in truth was large, considering your delicate frame. And Tom's disapproval was always blighting your mind. Like your mum's, who thought nail polish was enough, that skirts were enough. But we knew she only said that when her boyfriend side-eyed you.

With you, it was like being the python on the picket fence, causing offence to the neighbours. Our bodies sparkled like cyanide, and I'd wait, all cyan-eyed, for you to get off the fucking phone and look at how I looked at you. We'd watch the stars, circling in their fixed orbits. I'd watch them shine over you, thinking that despite the two-year difference in age, I wanted to be like you when I grew up. And when I thought for a moment, you'd notice that … while I wasn't impressive and that my kindness was enough … you'd go back to being the ficklest of suns.

Whomever your light happened to touch that day would feel the planets and stars align. But it was benign and when the light was gone, we'd be caved in by the darkness of the black hole you'd left us with. I know from experience: that November we didn't speak, for reasons unknown. You were so drunk on your cosmic power – of being the centre of everyone's universe – that I had to take you down from the sky, soften your grudge and tell you to give Tom a call. Not because I wanted you to. But because that 'commitment thing' was slipping.

Further into your illness you couldn't speak, and yet you were a figurine in a music box, twirling and twirling while everything around you grew thick with aching bones and opaqueness. You showed no interest in harnessing telomeres. In the past, you'd enjoy flirting with the notion that time was fleeting. Every cartwheel at twilight, every photoshoot on Brighton Pier, every golden hour cascading over your face. All finite. Doing one-last-times before knowing that was what they were.

I'm good with my words. You always said so. But I didn't do you justice at the funeral, 'cause after all, that's the point of loving someone: never having enough time in the world to say all that you want. The words we call the 'right' ones are hooked behind our lips until it's too late. Instead, I listed all the obscure music recommendations you gave me. The more subterranean the artist, the better. That's how you let your light shine in. But that open door I had in my heart for you has closed.

I feel fourteen again, balancing the breaking of my neurosis and the collapsing of my grandparents' minds. Rather than remain a prisoner and peel at my self-esteem, I'd leave my room in my school uniform every at 4:16 every morning. I'd walk along the sea wall, the coast blowing through my hair and *Ultraviolence* ringing in my ears, amplifying the thought that – at least in that moment – I was the most troubled kid who ever lived. The sun rose from the sea, and with it a cavalry of golden clouds.

I often reminisced about this when I looked into your eyes, thinking: what it would have been like, had we shared this moment together? To feel the tall grass beneath your bare feet, so soft it doesn't scratch your ankles? That was my place. The memory that I cherished whenever I walked into school with sweat around my collar. Now it is darkened by you and the cancer that took you from me.

I knew that if I made it as a writer, you would use your free signed copy as a doorstop. But it didn't matter. The polite nodding whenever I told you an idea was worth its weight in gold. Your gold. If you are somewhere close, in a changed nature, or in the echoes of a sea cave, I just hope you are living the way I knew you. No one holding the string to your kite. Your freedom made you unstoppable, even when the end lingered in your periphery. If you promise to be unapologetic, I promise to write about you one day, and the light you gave me. If I'm not too busy hiding in the remnants of the shadows you left behind.